Also by Nancy Willard

Poetry

Fiction

Short Story Collections

Short Stories and Essays

Critical Essays

Water Walker

WATER WALKER

by Nancy Willard

Drawings by John S. P. Walker

Alfred A. Knopf *New York* **1989**

THIS IS A BORZOI BOOK PUBLISHED BY ALFRED A. KNOPF, INC.

Copyright © 1972, 1982, 1984, 1987, 1988, 1989 by Nancy Willard

Illustrations copyright © 1989 by John Walker

All rights reserved under International and Pan-American Copyright
Conventions. Published in the United States by Alfred A. Knopf, Inc.,
and simultaneously in Canada by Random House of Canada Limited,
Toronto. Distributed by Random House, Inc., New York.

This book was completed with the help of a grant from The National
Endowment for the Arts.

All acknowledgments of previous publication of the poems in this
volume will be found at the end of the book.

Library of Congress Cataloging-in-Publication Data

Willard, Nancy.
  Water walker / Nancy Willard.
      p.   cm.
  ISBN 0-394-57208-4   ISBN 0-679-72171-1
(pbk.)
  I. Title.
PS3573.I444W38   1989
811'.54—dc19   88-25948
                      CIP

Manufactured in the United States of America

First Edition

for Alice and in memory of Martin

Best blessing of all is water.

—PINDAR, OLYMPIAN I

Contents

I

Water Walker

A Wreath to the Fish

Who is this fish, still wearing its wealth,
flat on my drainboard, dead asleep,
its suit of mail proof only against the stream?
What is it to live in a stream,
to dwell forever in a tunnel of cold,
never to leave your shining birthsuit,
never to spend your inheritance of thin coins?
And who is the stream, who lolls all day
in an unmade bed, living on nothing but weather,
singing, a little mad in the head,
opening her apron to shells, carcasses, crabs,
eyeglasses, the lines of fishermen begging for
news from the interior—oh, who are these lines
that link a big sky to a small stream
that go down for great things:
the cold muscle of the trout,
the shining scrawl of the eel in a difficult passage,
hooked—but who is this hook, this cunning
and faithful fanatic who will not let go
but holds the false bait and the true worm alike
and tears the fish, yet gives it up to the basket
in which it will ride to the kitchen
of someone important, perhaps the Pope
who rejoices that his cook has found such a fish
and blesses it and eats it and rises, saying,
"Children, what is it to live in the stream,
day after day, and come at last to the table,
transfigured with spices and herbs,
a little martyr, a little miracle;
children, children, who is this fish?"

The Feast of St. Tortoise

The day of her wedding, she crouches in the kitchen
and talks to the tortoise. He is older than she,
one of the family but celibate, reserved,

having taken holy orders in chapels of damp earth.
She admires his head, cobbled in ivory coins.

She touches his cowl, tender as chamois.
She praises his toadstool legs, his decisive beak,

and the raised ornament of his kindness
as he offers himself for a table

or a gameboard of fretted lacquer:
each hexagon fences a mound

into which a star has fallen so deeply
the whole field is on fire.

Let no guest go hungry.
She sets out a plate of lettuce chopped

into ruffles, the cool cheek
of an apple parceled and peeled.

This is for you, old friend.
He flippers forth. The bright worm of his tail
wags after him.

Psalm to the Newt

Look at the newt. He is worth watching.
The small stars of his hands sign the water.
His fingers thread beads of water on strands of water.

On the canopy of seaweed, he knits his proverbs:
Behold the newt—a weak arm may stir great secrets.
His arms, thin as threads, part curtains of water.
He is a rock to the snail and a snare to the worm.

His back raises an island: sad, a used tire.
The grainy dark of his skin glistens.
To the snails he brings the wet bark of trees.

Old shovel-head, guardian of patience,
you break through the silver roof
of the parliament of water
in the tiny pond of the aquarium.

You who sharpen your tail on the sunrise,
in your livery of cold flames you greet us,
in your vest buttoned with embers you greet us.

You turn on us, slowly, your hooded eyes.
Are you trying to change into something else
or change us into clouds,
shadowy behind glass as the lost gods?

Aquarium

The frog who works out
in the clean gym of the water

has neglected his arms.
Flexed, they are skinny as worms.

It's his legs he cares for,
plié perpetual,

muscles in baggy pants.
What charm when he extends

the ribbed fans of his feet,
as if a spider sat on a breath,

testing the weight of it.
Who in the corps of carp

or the schools of fantails
and angelfish, jewels

of the first water,
can match his leaps?

Airport Lobsters

Thrown together in a tank, a litter of lobsters
looks for the way back. When I hurry past, they wave
their taped claws—discreet, like the beaks of birds—
as if I were a door through which they could pass

to deep water, taking their leave of Atlantic shrimp in tins,
smoked oysters, caviar from the Caspian Sea.
My flight is late, and theirs will never arrive.
Their jet eyes pin regret on a watery map.

Moonstalkers, tidekeepers, robots of deep currents,
in whom indigo deepens to midnight when you give up
the ghost, forgive me. I won't forget the shoals of you,
the scrabbling heaps, the sick adrift, light lapping the dead

like a field of samurai in full armor,
your greaves freckled with ashes,
your corselets plated with moonlight,
your antennae still whipping

bubbles of pumped air.

Life at Sea: The Naming of Fish

Stand among fish and admire the angels,
the *Marble Angel,* like grillwork on a sad house
sunk in the suburbs of New Orleans,
and the *Black Angel,* little undertaker of the waters,
and the *Gold Angel,* new-minted, and the *Silver Angel*

that tumbles from God's purse and hides
Silver Dollars in the pockets of water,
their eyes in love with the shyness of pearls.
Schooled in silence, the catfish do not consider
you. *Glass Cats, Green Cats:* whiskered gentlemen,

they paddle to their clubs
in small expensive suits of woven jade.
The *Gold Convict* does not take flight,
though like a note in a bottle
it has lived its pale life in hiding.

What do we know of their risings and settings?
The *Red Oscar* wears twilight.
The *Black Lyre Tail* heads north,

a velvet arrow happily cutting the waves.
In the last tank, the *Blue Betta*

unfurls his fins, his silk bathrobe.
Like a lively invalid, he admires the tassels,
puts it on, takes it off, on, off,
and glides among branches of hornwort
under the mauve leaves of the purple krinkle.

He does not close his eyes when the sun falls
slow as a snail through the sky, and new moons
and old moons wish on the *Moon Platys,*
and the stars show us something familiar:
archer, lyre, hunter, dipper, fish.

Poem Made of Water

Praise to my text, Water, which taught me writing,
and praise to the five keepers of the text,
water in Ocean, water in River, water in Lake,
water in cupped hands, water in Tears. Praise
for River, who says: Travel to the source,
poling your raft of words, mindful of currents,
avoiding confusion, delighting in danger
when its spines sparkle, yet keeping
your craft upright, your sentence alive.
You have been sentenced to life.

Praise for Ocean and her generous lesson,
that a great poem changes from generation to generation,
that any reader may find his treasure there
and even the landlocked heart wants to travel.
Praise for that heart, for its tides,
for tiny pools winking in rocks
like poems which make much of small matters:
five snails, two limpets, a closely watched
minnow, his spine a zipper,
and a white stone wearing the handprints of dead coral.

Praise for Tears, which are faithful to grief
not by urns but by understatement.
Praise for thirst, for order in the eye and in the ear
and in the heart, and for water in cupped hands,

for the poem that slakes thirst
and the poem that wakes it.
Praise for Lake, which bustles with swimmers at noon.
I have been one, busy under the light,
piling rocks into castles, not seeing
my work under the ruffled water.

And later—the lake still sleepy in the last light—
the castle squats like the rough draft of a prayer,
disguised as a castle, which tells me
to peer into the dark and interpret shapes in the ooze:
the row boat rising like a beak, the oil drum rusting,
the pop bottles fisted in weeds, every sunken
thing still, without purpose, dreamed over
till the fisherman's net brings up—
what? a bronze mask? a torso of softest marble?

Go deep. Save, sift, pack, lose, find again.
Come back as snow, rain, tears, crest and foam.
Come back to baptize, heal, drown.
Come back as Water. Come back as Poem.

A Psalm for Running Water

Running water, you are remembered and called.
Physician of clover and souls; hock, glove
and slipper of stones.

Stitch thyme and buttercup to my boots.
Make me tread the psalm and sign of water
falling, when I am going the other way,
climbing the mountain for a clear view of home.

After winter's weeding and the fire's gap in the woods,
first ferns, trillium, watercress,
this vivid text, Water, shows your hand.

The trees stand so spare a child may write them.
You, Water, sing them like an old score,
settled, pitched soft and fresh,
and wash our wounds when we fall.

A hundred Baptists, hand in hand,
rise and fall in your body and rise again,
praising the Lord, Whose hand, I think, wears you.

For all this and more my great-grandmother
thumped out of bed on Easter and tramped
over gorse and thorn and wild thistle
to the water smiling through her husband's field.

She capped some in a cruet;
　　　the wink of God,
　　　the quick motion of ourselves in time,
　　　flashing! flashing!

II

The Road

In Praise of Unwashed Feet

Because I can walk over hot coals,
because I can make doctors turn green
and shoe salesmen avert their eyes,
because I have added yet another use
to the hundred and one uses of Old Dutch Cleanser;
because they tell me the secrets of miners and small boys,
because they keep me in good standing and continual grace
in the ashes and dust of the last rites,
because they carry my great bulk without complaint,
because they don't smell;
because it's taken me years
to grow my own shoes, like the quaint signatures of truth,
because they are hard and gentle as lion's pads,
pard's paw, mule's hoof and cock's toes,
because they can't make poems or arguments
but speak in an aching tongue or not at all
and come home at night encrusted with stones,
calluses, grass, all that the head forgets
       and the foot knows.

A Hardware Store As Proof
of the Existence of God

I praise the brightness of hammers pointing east
like the steel woodpeckers of the future,
and dozens of hinges opening brass wings,
and six new rakes shyly fanning their toes,
and bins of hooks glittering into bees,

and a rack of wrenches like the long bones of horses,
and mailboxes sowing rows of silver chapels,
and a company of plungers waiting for God
to claim their thin legs in their big shoes
and put them on and walk away laughing.

In a world not perfect but not bad either
let there be glue, glaze, gum, and grabs,
caulk also, and hooks, shackles, cables, and slips,
and signs so spare a child may read them,
Men, Women, In, Out, No Parking, Beware the Dog.

In the right hands, they can work wonders.

The Unspeakable Telephone

"My father, he always adored the telephone.
He loved to call weather and time. These days
if you have a phone, you can talk to anything.

And once we were walking the beach together
at Provincetown, on the wettest day of the season,
the waves burst like bombs at our feet,
I was certain the sky was falling,

and my father said, 'Look! A telephone!'
All alone on the beach it stood,
like a flower on a stem, no shelter at all,
not even the convenience of a directory.

My father said, 'Let us ring for a taxi.'
I said, 'It won't work, not way out here.
Father, you're eighty-two,
even a cold at your age can be fatal.'

But he never listened, he plucked the receiver
and pushed in a dime and dialed.
The coastguard was blowing hundreds of whistles.
How many boats went down in that storm?
'Let's go!' I shouted. 'The phone is broken.'

Just then the receiver gurgled,
and my father smiled and raised his head.
'I can hear perfectly.'"

Coming to the Depot

They are just married, and is he surprised,
he who rode this train with one bag and a beer
and silence when he wanted it and his own speech.

He stares at his wife.
Where did all these bags come from?
What's in them? She is taking out

shampoos, conditioners, creams,
wiping the bottles and muttering,
"Ziploc bags. You forgot the Ziploc bags."

Now she is combing her hair,
feeling for rollers, curlers, and pins.
He says, "We're coming into the depot."

"You mean station," she says. "Not depot."
"Depot," he says. She smiles.
"Where I come from you would never hear that."

"Depot," he says. "Depot."
"I heard that once in a movie," she says.
Feather clips chained to the gold clips

on her ears, sharp rings on both hands,
her hands waving, the nail polish drying,
and a woman who was once beautiful

lurches down the aisle fighting
a diaper bag and a baby,
everyone is eating chicken or chewing gum,

and beyond the window, the milkweed blows.
It's twilight. I was a seed once, he thinks.
I was a seed. It was that easy.

In the Stretch Limousine

"Climb in," said a voice, and I stepped down
into a velvet pit so dark and vast
I fell into the left hand of God, a place with no
lights, yet hammered and hemmed in light.

On the horizon the driver shadowed the faint helm
of the moon and gathered the night around him.
"Push that button to your left," he called,
and I did, and the floor cracked open like a grave,

as if the spirits wanted to look
me over before sending up a bottle of gin,
half empty, and three dirty glasses.
"Try the phone," he called, and I did.

I could hardly hear him. I believed he could not hear me.
When I said, "Where are we?" the phone went dead.
Finally I caught his voice, so far off
he might have been crossing Africa,

watching delicate horned beasts unfold
a single sentence: "You want the stars?"
The roof lifted itself like an animal waking,
and a page turned in the Book of Life.

When everything stopped and I climbed out,
he said no more to me than I would say
to a star that was falling to earth
the day it was born and finally made it home.

Science Fiction

Here, said the spirit,
is the Diamond Planet:
Shall I change you into a diamond?
No? Then let us proceed
to the Red Planet
desert star,
rocks too young to know
lichens. There's plenty
of room. Stay as long
as you like. You don't like?
Then let us go forth to
the Planet of Mists,
the veiled bride,
the pleasures of losing and finding,
the refinement of symbols.
She's all yours.

I see you looking at that blue planet.
It's mostly water.
The land's crowded with
creatures. You have mists
but they rain, diamonds
but they cost. You have
only one moon.
You have camels and babies and cigars
but everything grows up
or wears out.
And on clear nights
you have the stars
without having them.

III

The Garden

Walking Poem

How beautifully the child I carry on my back
teaches me to become a horse.
How quickly I learn to stay
between shafts, blinders, and whips,
bearing the plough

and the wagon loaded with hay,
or to break out of trot and run
till we're flying through cold streams.
He who kicks my commands
knows I am ten times his size

and that I am servant to small hands.
It is in mowed fields I move best,
watching the barn grow toward me,
the child quiet, his sleep piled like hay
on my back as we slip over the dark hill

and I carry the sun away.

Cat Rising Among the Angels

(for Tracy Gallup)

The artist who sees angels
makes a cat. She names the cat
Angel. She puts a fish
in his pocket and a mask
on his face and sends him away.
The mask makes the cat invisible

to birds, fish, cats, invisible
to everyone but angels.
He longs for wings. Something chips away
at his huge hunger, the hunger of a cat
to taste everything, to mask
his shadow, float like a fish.

He no longer dreams of eating fish
but of higher things, invisible
provisions. Has his feathered mask
made him one of the angels,
winged, holy, the first cat
to send the birds and mice away?

Shall the meek inherit the earth? Far away
by the River of Life, the guardian angels fish
for the souls about to be born. The cat
paddles among them, his appetite invisible,
of course, to the angels,
till his mortal mask

slips. Meanwhile the artist who made the mask
is sorry she gave it away.
How she would love to walk among angels
with a cat who makes amulets of fish
and women with fish tails, invisible
to angels but not to the cat.

The artist calls and calls her faithless cat.
Meanwhile the angels can scarcely mask
their amazement. "A whiskered moon, half invisible,
swimming among the saved! Can we turn it away?"
The artist disguises herself as a fish
and sets off for heaven shouting, "Angels!

Return my cat! I sent him away
with the wrong mask and the wrong fish.
He is invisible and dangerous only to angels!"

Small Medicinal Poem

Only that which is truly oneself
has the power to heal.

—CARL JUNG

With the ears of a deer I hear your story,
how you followed your father to the mountain,
how you followed him through juniper and birch,
how you found the clearing sacred to the deer people,
how their hooves printed hollow hearts in the mud,
how your father followed their prints,
how you dragged your feet,
how a hawk drew high circles around you,
how you looked away when your father said,
These are fresh tracks. Aim for the heart.

With the eyes of a hawk I see your story,
your father waiting for you to fire
at the doe who twitched into the clearing,
her fur slick with light, her ears pointing north.
You took aim at someone you wanted to wish on,
as welcome a guest as the first star.
Your father who loves you hissed, *Now! Now!*
And I think when you lowered your gun, half-weeping,
you found your own space. You became what you are.

With the tongue of a star, you tell me your story,
full of silence and distance and inner space.
What shall we call you in this chapter?
"He Who Cannot Eat Chicken Without Grieving."
"He Who Has Fallen in Love with the Moon."
"The Curate of Cats Who Has Understood Purring."
"He Whose Cat Spied a New Star and Told No One."
"He Who Carries a Glass Wand That Does Nothing."
"The Doctor of Divinities Who Have Fallen from Grace,"
or, in the language of the deer people: *he who saves.*

For Karen

She who came thousands of miles to say goodbye
sits in the plain room by her father's body.
It is her father and not her father
in the red-checked shirt her mother sent
like a birthday gift to the hushed house of the dead.
Terrible, saying goodbye to this flesh that can't hear,
to this mouth that can't answer.
Terrible, that a husband and wife linked
by thousands of days in the long light
of the studio where the only words spoken
flowed from each other as back and forth
they passed the paintings that deepened
under their hands and gathered themselves into books—
terrible that such parents should lose each other.
A week before her wedding, how terrible to be happy!
But she can't forget how her father loved to read
the night away and in the morning greet her,
"What do you think of this book? Isn't it
wonderful?" She pages through the good
times. He knows the ending.
Still, she tells him the whole story.

Ilse's Sleep

In Bangall, in a house in a forest, how patiently
Ilse waits for sleep, a shy animal, to arrive.
How everything frightens it. The breath of a bird
at three, the crack of a twig at four.
She in whom cats confide cannot call it.
She who applauds the moon's rising, she who draws
the moon from a well and sprinkles moonwater
on the one hundred and two pots of anemones

in her garden, cannot draw it.
What is to be done? Her husband reads to her.
Poems. Novels. History. What does her sleep
know of history? His voice swabs away letters
unwritten, tasks undone. His voice cleanses,
folds, puts away. When her sleep arrives,
it looks over its shoulder for the secret
police and licks its wounds from the dark

days in Berlin, days of making paper
and printing passports for Jews,
hidden like stars at noon; horses
dead in the streets; a dead boy leaning
against an apple tree blossoming
for the girl whose sleep saw everything
and buried it, but carries it to her now,
in a house in a forest, in Bangall.

Marriage Amulet

You are polishing me like old wood.
At night we curl together like two rings
on a dark hand. After many nights,
the rough edges wear down.

If this is aging, it is warm as fleece.
I will gleam like ancient wood.
I will wax smooth, my crags and cowlicks
well-rubbed to show my grain.

Some sage will keep us in his hand for peace.

A Psalm for Vineyards

In the aging cellars, the wines are settling down.
Spirits destined to age in oak sleep
in cool barrels, their curved backs rising like loaves,
sauvignon blanc, sémillon, merlot
ripening, rack on rack. From the footbridge
spanning their stillness, I can see everything

and nothing. Twilight was born here.
What do spirits know of the world above?
The vineyards' calligraphy? The contredances
of vine clasping vine? Hawks riding the wind
over stands of acacia? The cellist
on the terrace above who fastens *Bach's Greatest Hits*

with a clothespin and closes his eyes and plays?
They have survived the crushpit, the auger,
and fermentation to something less than themselves.
Born again, clarified, they go back to the world.
In the hives hidden under the plum trees, silence
is sealed in cells. I would feel at home there.

Bedtime Story

Her married son lies in his old bed,
his suitcase sprawled on the floor.
Downstairs, his mother locks the door.
He hears the knob turn—clack!—and her small steps,
like a wounded bird flopping its way to freedom,
hears them stop on the stairs and turn back.
She has forgotten what called her forth
and from the landing calls,
"I'm going to check the door," and stands
at the locked door and asks, "Is everyone in?
Hal, Lizzie, Margaret—what can be keeping them?"
Your son will know, says the door. He did so well
on his exams, he must know everything.
She turns on his light to admire him.
He blinks at her like a peeved owl. "Dead.
They're all dead. Go to sleep, Mother."
She glides to her room. She almost climbs into bed.
But what does he know? She knows they are in the house.
She peers into every room, taps every light.
Though she feels their names waking,
though she hears their steps taking flight
and their minute adjustments of deadbolt and latch,
those missing in action shall remain so.
She stands still. She keeps the morning watch.

The Teachings of the Jade

The jade tree is all thumbs,
green ones. What she couldn't grow
if she had a mind to!

Admirer of elephants
and oaks, venerable
mathematician of the greenhouse

constructing proofs so vast
she's forgotten the problem
and given herself to

abstruse branches of knowledge,
speaking in thick tongues,
urging emerald ears for mice

and knees that don't bend;
with mineral patience, she takes
her time, would make room

for me, if I were new enough
to know my place
under the family tree.

Roots

This squash is my good cousin,
says the vegetable man,
rolling his pushcart through November.

These parsnips are first class.
I recommend with my whole heart.
I know the family.

Believe me, lady, I know
what I'm talking.
And I give you a good price.

I throw in the carrots free.
Carrots like this you got?
So what you want?

I wrap in the best Yiddish newspaper.
A dollar a year. Takes me
ten minutes to read it,

an hour to read the English.
Potatoes you need, maybe?
My wife says I eat too many

potatoes. In Poland, in war,
we ate potatoes, soup,
baked, boiled.

All my family was ploughed under
except me. So what can I say
to someone that he don't like

potatoes? Positively last chance,
because tomorrow it might snow.
In winter I don't come.

Look for me when the snow goes,
and if I don't come back,
think that I moved, maybe.

I'm eighty-two already,
and what is Paradise
without such potatoes?

Onionlight

Sacks crammed with light, layer on luminous layer,
an underworld calendar, the peeled pages faintly lined
but printed without month or measure
and pure as the damp kiss of a pearl,

as if the rings in an old tree should suddenly separate
and bracelet the axe; I have stooped among onions all morning,
hunting these flightless birds as they perched among roots.
I have yanked them out by the tail

and dropped them into my bag like chickens
and pulled away the thin paper of their last days,
pale winegold, a silken globe, pungent,
striped with the pale longitude of silence.

Now over my door they shimmer in knobby garlands,
gregarious in chains like a string of lights
on the boardwalks of heaven where an old man
who loved his garden understands everything.

The Potato Picker

The plant lifts easily now, like an old tooth.
I can free it from the rows of low hills,
hills like the barrows of old kings

where months ago, before anything grew or
      was,
we hid the far-sighted eyes of potatoes.
They fingered forth, blossomed, and shrank,

and did their dark business under our feet.
And now it's all over. Horse nettles dangle
their gold berries. Sunflowers, kindly giants,

in their death-rattle, turn stiff as streetlamps.
Pale cucumbers swell to alabaster lungs,
while marigolds caught in the quick frost

go brown, and the scarred ears of corn
      gnawed
by the deer lie scattered like primitive fish.
The life boats lifted by milkweed ride light

and empty, their sailors flying.
This is the spot. I put down my spade,
I dig in, I uncover the scraped knees

of children in the village of potatoes,
and the bald heads of their grandfathers.
I enter the potato mines.

The Weeder

Under the ground, all those voices:
the wet worm slipples past roots and opens tunnels,
grubs shiver in sunlight like sucked thumbs,
the locust splits his armor, goes forth a civilian,
and the roots tangle and clasp each other
like the hairs of a sleeper, hugging so hard
not even a big-toothed comb can part them.

By hand and by trowel I have picked my way
through the birth-rooms of weeds,
and the sleeping and waking of flowers,
and the roots of violets cracking their knuckles.
The lily of the valley lays down its life in miles
of pale cable, sending at intervals its green report.

When I get to the root of the matter,
the fat fingers of irises flash their soft blades
like the tail feathers of remarkable birds,
and the peonies turn on their taproots stained with sunset—
sherrydark corks that have ripened in deep cellars.
Galaxies of bulbs are rolling themselves into pearls.

I have dug, snipped, pulled, fed, taken, thrown away,
and what do the roots give me? Year after year they surrender
toy soldiers old children have lost in the grass.
Men of plastic, they do not become the grass.
This one hauls his machine gun under the roses;
gripped by its roots, he is taking aim at the dark.

Preserves

To lift the crisp crust of the earth,
to slip under its eaves bulb after bulb
like pale bellies carrying astonishing children:
Silver Trumpet, Chicago Petticoats, My Hope,
Rainbow Breeder's Mixture, Blue Parrot, Angels' Tears—

lilies holding their breath on thin wands,
tulips bearing their secret black stars,
daffodils, gold gossips of the garden—

To tamp the roof over them, plunging them
into darkness, to set flask after flask
with their brown wrappers curling and crumbling
into the pharmacopoeia of the earth
and the tangled sleep of fennel, catnip,

hyssop, and sage— To leave them there,
small sacks of ivory, which when split
hold themselves together, giving me shares

of smooth stock: I have invested in good company.
Upstairs where I live the pine drops its needles.
They rust the air, they rest on the earth like the fur
of some vast shorn animal that shivers itself to sleep.
The catalpa drops everything, blows
clumsy hearts on its bed.

God Enters the Swept Field

A field in ruins. Everything's coming due:
a scarf of starlings rinsing itself in the air,

pumpkins like quilted planets closing down,
coins tumbling out of the poplars' high rooms,

a party of maples basting an amber beast,
done to a turn on their black boughs. God's brooms

on hills honey-brushed and glowing like new loaves
scour and scrub the weeds, beaten thin and bright.

Let in the light.

Memorial Day
in Union City, Michigan

At noon an angel was seen in my grandmother's kitchen,
seen by Maria M———, of sound mind, clear sight.
Hulling the strawberries, tossing their crowns to the sink,
she felt "eyes on me, watching," and turned. Its gaze
rested on the turkey—bare-chested under the basting,
wings lacquered with butter and sharp as elbows—
as if it wondered how birds allow themselves to be
      caught.

At one o'clock, in the front bedroom, the angel appeared
to my grandmother. She had just lain down for a nap.
"Unwary, like those extinct birds you read about,
who gave their killers a kind of welcome."
It looked in the dresser mirror a long time,
astonished at what it found, another room,
another grandmother, another angel.

At three o'clock the gardener saw a figure
standing on top of the compost and found himself
filled with such longing for another time and condition
he burst into tears. "I thought it was a sleepwalker."
He followed it to the forsythia, lost it to silence
and yellow bells. All afternoon, spading the new plot,
he felt as if he were digging his own grave.

From four till ten, the angel was not seen at all,
but for once in our world, everybody was happy.
I was six years old and no one called me for bed.
My deaf cat purred and purred by my dark window.
In the happy silence of a parade departed,
the forgotten dead accepted our forgiveness,
still air throbbing, distant pulse of a drum.

Little Elegy
with Books and Beasts

in memory of Martin Provensen (1916–1987)

I

Winters when the gosling froze to its nest
he'd warm it and carry it into the house praising
its finely engraved wings and ridiculous beak—
or sit all night by the roan mare, wrapping
her bruised leg, rinsing the cloths while his wife
read aloud from *Don Quixote,* and darkness hung
on the cold steam of her breath—
or spend five days laying a ladder for the hen
to walk dryshod into the barn.

Now the black cat broods on the porch.
Now the spotted hound meeting visitors, greets none.
Nestler, nurse, mender of wounded things,
he said he didn't believe in the body.
He lost the gander—elder of all their beasts
(not as wise as the cat but more beloved)—
the night of the first frost, the wild geese
calling—last seen waddling south
on the highway, beating his clipped wings.

II

He stepped outside through the usual door
and saw for the last time his bare maples
scrawling their cold script on the low hills
and the sycamore mottled as old stone
and the willows slurred into gold by the spring light,
and he noticed the boy clearing the dead brush—

old boughs that broke free under the cover of snow,
and he raised his hand, and a door in the air opened,
and what was left of him stumbled and fell
and lay at rest on the earth like a clay lamp
still warm whose flame was not nipped or blown
but lifted out by the one who lit it
and carried alive over the meadow—
that light by which we read, while he was here,
the chapter called Joy in the Book of Creation.

IV

Songs

The Goose, the Fox, and the Snake
Advise a Rabbit

"What's wanted," said the greedy goose,
"is crackled corn, served fast and loose.
Spring water, taken through a straw,
sends lovely shivers down your craw.
Ten heaping tablespoons will make
a quick end to your stomach ache."

The fox with furrowed fur drew near
and whispered in the rabbit's ear.
"The stomach of a goose is tough
but we are made of finer stuff.
And fat of goose—especially good
when carried through a starlit wood
and seethed all night in skin of snake—
will cure the strongest stomach ache."

The snake hissed high, the snake hissed low.
"A little venom from my fangs
will put an end to all your pangs,
the stuffy nose, the splitting head,
the sting that racks, the chill that shakes.
It ends, of course, all stomach aches."
She brushed her tooth against his toe.
She pressed her smile against the bone.

The rabbit fled.
The ache was gone.

The Cat to His Dinner

Fern and flower, safely keep
this tender mouse I put to sleep.

Let snow and silence mark the site
of my unseemly appetite.

Her bravery, her tiny fall
shall be a model for us all.

May God, Who knows our best and worst,
send me another as good as the first.

A Cautionary Tale

Said the cat to the mole, "How dreadful
to be so exceedingly small!
With claws good for nothing but digging
and teeth good for nothing at all.
And fur as plain
as the wind and the rain,
and eyes sealed up like a wall."

Said the mole to the cat, "Never follow
friends with hooks at the ends of their paws.
Not for worlds would I bring home to dinner
a guest wearing knives in her jaws.
What need have I
of the lamps in the sky?
I carry a star on my nose."

Said the cat to the mole—but who knows
what answer he might have given?
A dog flashed over the field.
Now the cat, caterwauling heaven,
looks down on the mole,
snug in her hole,
small as a rose,
black as a barge.
"I thank my stars
I am dark and low
and not large."

The Games of Night

The ghost comes. I don't see her.
I smell the licorice drops in her pocket.
I climb out of bed, I draw her bath.
She has come a long way, and I know she's tired.

By the light of the moon, the water splashes.
By the light of the stars, the soap leaps,
it dives, it pummels the air,
it scrubs off the dust of not-seeing,

and I see her sandals, black like mine.
and I see her dress, white like mine.
Little by little, she comes clear.
She rises up in a skin of water.

As long as the water shines, I can see her.
As long as I see her, we can play
by the light of the moon on my bed,
by the light of the stars on my bear
till the sun opens its eye, the sun that wakes things,
the sun that doesn't believe in ghosts.

Magic Story for Falling Asleep

When the last giant came out of his cave
and his bones turned into the mountain
and his clothes turned into the flowers,

nothing was left but his tooth
which my dad took home in his truck
which my granddad carved into a bed

which my mom tucks me into at night
when I dream of the last giant
when I fall asleep on the mountain.

Night Song

Farewell child
and farewell lamp

cats that wait
at hearth and hole

farewell mole
and farewell bones

thief at gate
and fire on stones

farewell owl
farewell lark—

farewell dark.

Two Songs:
An Exchange with Peter Beagle

The Magician (Willard)

All hot and cold with fever,
wrapped in her husband's coat,
She said, "I see Saint Michael
rowing my father's boat."

Her husband the magician
piled blankets on the bed.
She said, "I see my mother,
she's throwing me a thread."

Her husband the magician
canceled his matinees,
and from his net he scattered
a skein across her gaze.

She said, "If I cross over
this river, I shall die."
He knelt and drank the river,
he sucked the fever dry.

She said, "I see the sparrows
and plums of paradise."
Out of his hat he ordered
apples and doves and mice

to rub against her hands,
wasting against the sheet.
She said, "I smell the planets,
they're burning at my feet,

and time is burning slowly,
a slowly blackening flower."
He danced upon the bedstead,
he sang upon the hour,

dark as the nighttime hat
in which all tricks begin,
which orders forth the sparrow
and calls it back again.

With bread and milk he wooed her,
ashes and weddings, sewed
together in his mutterings
as through the woods they rode

beating the woods together
until he knew they'd won,
and felt upon his wrist
the tamed and hooded sun.

Magicians' Wives (Beagle)

Magicians go in scarlet,
damson and verdigris,
their hoods and cloaks and smiles
asnap with wizardry.
Magicians' wives wear brown,
and they're very hard to see.
                    Magicians' wives, magicians' wives.

Magicians weave great circles
Where demons are confined,
buzzing like horseflies, helpless
in the meshwork of the mind.
Magicians' wives clean up the mess
the demons left behind.
                    Magicians' wives, magicians' wives.

Sweet are the ladies of the Shi.
Dryads are kind, or seem to be.
The wisest are the women of the waters.
Witches have useful things to teach—
the hidden names and the secret speech—
but magicians always marry gardeners' daughters.
                    Magicians' wives, magicians' wives.

Magicians study colors
and learn the names of elves
in lion-smelling towers
where grimoires line the shelves.
Magicians' wives bear children

and watch them hurt themselves.
                    Magicians' wives, magicians' wives.

Magicians know what time is
and know its antidote.
They read the past in snakeskin,
the future in a mote.
Magicians' wives wash crucibles
and buy another goat.
                    Magicians' wives, magicians' wives.

On certain nights without a name
magicians gather at a flame
to speak of string and stones and stars and weather.
They draw strange pictures on the floor,
trade palindromes and rhymes of lore,
and things you do with marigold, rue and heather.
                    Magicians' wives, magicians' wives.

The wives sit in the kitchen,
replenishing the beer.
They fold and sew and giggle
and call each other "dear."
And now and then they make
somebody's husband disappear.
                    Magicians' wives, magicians' wives.

V

Saints Lose Back
(The Poems Behind the Headlines)

"Saints Lose Back"

And there was complacency in heaven
for the space of half an hour,
and God said, Let every saint lose his back.

Let their wings and epaulettes shrivel,
and for immortal flesh give them flesh of man,
and for the wind of heaven a winter on earth.

The saints roared like the devil.
O my God, cried Peter, what have you done?
And God said,

Consider the back,
the curse of backache
the humpback's prayer.

Consider how thin a shell man wears.
The locust and crab are stronger than he.
Consider the back, how a rod breaks it.

Now consider the front, adorned with eyes,
cheeks, lips, breasts, all
the gorgeous weaponry of love.

Then consider the back, good for nothing
but to fetch and carry, crouch and bear
and finally to lie down on the earth.

O, my angels, my exalted ones,
consider the back,
consider how the other half lives.

"Buffalo Climbs Out of Cellar"

"Will you have some sherry?" asked
the million-dollar baby-faced killer.

He filled my glass, and the whole room
sucked me into its sharkish smile.

"You're fond of hunting," I said.
"Did you shoot all those guys on the wall?"

He nodded and raised the cuff of his pants.
His left leg was ivory to the knee.

"That Bengal tiger was my first success.
Then I matched wits with a white whale

and won. After that I went in for elephants.
And then I heard about the last buffalo

in South Dakota. Very educated.
He speaks fluent Apache. He writes

by scratching his hooves in the dirt.
He's writing a history of the Civil War.

So naturally I took him alive. Day
and night I keep him locked in my cellar.

His breath heats this house all winter.
His heart charges all my rooms with light.

In my worst dreams I see them folding up
like a paper hat, and my dead tiger roaring

and my dead whale swimming off the wall
and my buffalo climbing out of the cellar."

"Giants Meet Reviving Eagles on Monday Night"

Landlord, I've got to move.
You didn't tell me the guys upstairs
are thirty feet tall and could carry
this whole house on their brass knuckles.
You didn't say that next door
lives a sect of bald-headed eagles
who burn themselves every night
and every morning rise from the dead.
I can sleep through the crashing and cawing,
my pictures dropping, my windows snored out.
But the eagles are planning a big revival,
and the giants are giving a party tomorrow night,
and I'm giving notice.
They don't mess with me.
They even asked me to come,
but I'm allergic to feathers,

and I never drink anything stronger than blood.

"Tigers Shake Up Pitchers Again"

First God made the waters of heaven.
Then he made two pitchers to hold it.
Then he said to his angel,

When I call for rain, dip rain from the sky
and pour it out on the fields of men.
From the gold pitcher comes plenty.
From the silver pitcher comes terror.

The angel was eager, slim, and alarmed.
How shall I, who am without weight
lift the pitchers that water the world?

Then God made two tigers.
He named the silver one thunder.
He named the gold one lightning
and loosed them both in the villages of the stars.

He made the flesh of the stars a poison.
He made the tigers strong and thirsty.
Listen to them, listen to them,
drunk with thirst, shaking the jugs of heaven.

Can you hear the wrath of silver?
Can you see the whips of gold?
Can you feel the rain on your face at last?

"Foxes Fall to St. Francis"

"Religion," said the foxes,
"is for the birds.

And that man in the brown gown
is a hunter. Watch out."

The sparrows watched him
bake bread and sow crumbs

and the snow kept falling.
He seemed too weak

to make a meal of sparrows
and too dumb.

No claws, no beak,
a nest without young.

He trapped roots, berries,
chestnuts,

and the snow kept falling
(also the sun).

Many birds drew near
and admired his peculiar singing,

and he kept scattering seeds,
and badgers and hares drew

themselves up
to his stone table.

He ate only his words.
The snow kept falling

on the food,
on the far-off dead,

on paths paved
with mercy.

The foxes said,
"What's good enough for birds

is good enough."
And they fell on the feast

and were saved.

"Angels Shade Vida"

When the sun breaks over the desert
other people fight back with tents and turbans,
polarized glasses and sad houseboys with fans.
Only Vida has angels to shade him.

I don't think he's any better than I am.
I don't think God loves him more than me
or more than the president of Coca-Cola
or the assassin who sharpens his knife on injustice.

And then I see him going down the street
with a hundred wings wheeling over his head
and incense of myrrh and peppermint fanning the air,
and a hundred halos to light the way at night,

and I ask, who is Vida that he deserves so much?
and why does only God see the just man in disguise,
and if all this is the grace of God,
why doesn't it ever happen to me?

"Roach Paces North Stars"

Earth fell
(the last man,
last woman,
last child

into ashes, gossip
for rivers,
mortar for sticks
and stones)

to the small guerrillas
of the kitchen.
The roach goes to bed
in his armor,

has all the time
in the world and nothing
to spend it on,
and no estate more

real than his dark
cold cave
under all-seeing heaven
where the roach-gods

take their pleasure,
dozing by day,
lighting fires night
after night

where one roach
from the dead earth

arrives
in a rocket

small as a vitamin,
certain as arsenic,
fire-thief risen
from the low life.

"Giants Anxious for Skins"

They wanted to swim in the raw,
to slough off
their warts and bristles,
bruises and tough
talk. And scars.

They hid their skins
in a brake of ferns
and wrapped what remained
in scarves of water.
The skins grieved

and gave themselves to
the first comers,
the shifty rocks
and their promises:
Cleave to us.

Your bristles shall be bushes,
your warts sapphires,
your bruises lichens.
In your scars will shine
mushrooms and moths.

Let the giants stay
restless but clean to the bone,
carrying travelers
or drowning them.

"Angels' Singer Stops Orioles"

In May the orioles arrived,
staked out their lands,
stitched nests like pockets
in the coats of the trees
where their eggs,
priceless as souls,
hid in those purses
blowing and bobbing
like seeds rocked in
languorous fruit.

With song the orioles
surveyed their boundaries,
with song pushed them
east, west, etc.
into the no-direction
of heaven.
And the Lord heard
the clatter of wings
feathered in sunrise
and starless nights.

And the Lord called an angel
from the ranks of the blessed
to stop them,
to mark the meeting
of yes and no
of quick and dead
not with a line that might
lose its way
but a song.
No one on earth hears

that song
but the dying.
They listen,
their throats rattle:
coins shaken from a purse,
the beating of wings—
their clatter and shine—
breaking on silence.

"Stone Leads Ladies Golf"

See the small stone on the green,
white as a golf ball.

To children she shows herself as a pearl.
To dogs she rises up as a bone.

The lady takes off her glasses and swings.
Believe me, lovers of the low score,

the meek shall inherit the earth.
The ball shall lie down by the club,

and a little stone shall lead them.

"Four Seeds Defeated at Wimbledon"

The green man said, Choose me.
I hold in my fist four seeds.

Plant them tonight.
Tomorrow, harvest an army.

The boy traded his cow for the seeds.
At dawn he saw them, raising

their thorns, their deadly fruit,
their poisonous handshakes.

Who could withstand such might?
Then he saw far off a gang of mowers.

The green man said, Choose me.
They bear the weapon of death,

we bear the weapon of sleep.
They have feet and run fast,

we have roots and run slow.
Not even the stones know we are winning.

"Giant Streak Snarls Race"

I was running the last lap well
when all of a sudden I see
this guy sneak up behind me.
No, I never saw him before.
No, he wasn't on anyone's team.
He had white hair like fireworks,
he had wheels instead of legs,
six pairs of wings and too many eyes.
Well, I kicked his front wheel
and wrestled him to the ground,
and that's why we had a pileup.
I swear to God he turned into a cloud,
and now I've got this gamey leg.
When my good leg wants to rest,
it wants to walk on the top of the mountain.
The mountain? Who asked for the mountain?
All I asked was to keep in shape.

"Field Collapses Behind Patullo"

The First Scroll

To the chief eunuch of her Imperial Majesty
Marco Polo said,

"My country lies under yours.
If you dig a hole in your garden
you'll find me feeding the birds in mine.
Farewell!"

In the fourth moon, he weeded the lotus pond.
In the seventh moon, he cut the chrysanthemums.
In the ninth moon he covered their roots for the
          winter.
Farewell!

West of the Jade Girdle Bridge,
north of the Gate of White Peonies,
he dug a way out
from the ten thousand peacocks wanting their own way,

from the lotus, twisting its feet in the shallows
and the lizards like jokes cracked by an emerald.

Farewell.

The Second Scroll

When this eunuch died, another replaced him.
He, too, dug quietly toward the promised land.
The eunuch of the twenty-fifth generation
barely remembered the story.

What did he know of Marco Polo?
What did he know of New Jersey

and Patullo the chicken farmer, profoundly unlucky,
who on the sixth hour of the seventh moon

quarreled with his wife
and stomped toward the barn, with her calling
Go to hell
as the shovel broke through like a tooth

and the whole field collapsed behind him?

"Ailing Stomach Delays Swan"

Over the moat, round as a teething ring,
flew snow geese and swans and larks.

The great swan heard them.
"Time to get up," said his wife.

He thought of the cold streams of heaven,
the swamps where they'd bed down,

their feet hooked in the ice,
their food hidden by frost

and never enough for all.
"Time to get up," said his wife.

He thought of the inner circle,
the cozy castle,

the feasts among friends.
Rinds, pickles, pomegranates.

He thought: how much men throw away!
Next day his wife was gone.

The king's cook tossed out
gristle from the great table,

bones of capons,
the gnawed breast of a lark.

The great swan ate to keep his strength up.
Overstuffed, a masked sofa,

he took to the air,
dodged arrows, wheeled his wings

and lifted his dead weight
toward his brothers whose leavings

he still tasted,
tired now, and sick of the whole family.

"Wayward Lass Wins Mother Goose"

"Good for nothing but sleeping late
and sleeping around," said Humanmother,

"and for dropping her suitors like stitches
and for singing off key with the cats

and for sitting on eggs and letting
the hens take their ease, and for

skipping with lambs instead of
shearing them and running

with water instead of fetching it
home from the well."

"Let her sleep in the sty," said Humanfather.
"Let her gossip with ganders."

And they turned her out into the yard
and she lay in the straw, listening,

and Goosemother sang,
"O, my wild flower, my featherless daughter,

I bless your tongue and its wayward verses,
I bless your mouth and its burden of nonsense.

I give you my faith in the kindness of butchers
and my foolishness, which has made me immortal.

I give you the keys to my queer kingdom."

"Nets Halt Suns"

In those days there were
two suns.

All-father rose in the east.
All-mother rose in the west.

At noon they rested
and admired the earth,

the rain, the leaves falling,
windfall apples in tall grass,

and our ancestors
falling into bed

or gravely falling
asleep forever,

the dust rolling over them
in slow motion.

When the suns went down,
darkness fell after them.

O, to fall into life,
to fall down, to be human!

It was noon when they left
the road of heaven.

It was noon when they fell,
hissing and spitting.

All the grass curled up.
All creatures hid themselves,

in rocks, in caves,
save one old man.

He'd been trawling all day
and caught nothing.

He had nothing to lose.
He spread his nets

and they tossed All-father
to the wide sky

and they caught All-mother
and the sea took her

and gave to all water
her ten thousand faces.

"Sun Accused of Illegal Purchases"

A window shopper all his life,
he made arrangements for a wife.

He paid her husband fifty jars
of northern lights and giant stars,

a handsome acreage of sky,
an undiscovered galaxy,

and other things he did not own.
She would be his and his alone.

"O blazing love! Light of my life!"
He quite consumed his little wife,

who perished of appalling burns
but reappeared by fits and turns

and shows her husband, safe in bed,
her constellation overhead.

"Stars Nip Wings"

"Sun and moon go down, my dear.
What matters when they rise?
The falcon bears us all away,
the beautiful, the wise,
and none returns to tell the rest
where that creature flies."

"Sun and moon will hatch, my dear,
and the stars nip our wings,
if ever I forget my love,
the lowly sparrow sings.
Can you and I do less, my dear,
than simple, lawless things?"

"Divine Child Rolls On"

Lullaby, my sparrow.
Cipher, make your mark
in the Book of Being.
Fly into the dark,

passenger of the planet.
Sun and stars are gone.
The Divine Child find you,
bless you, and roll on.

A Note About the Author

Nancy Willard grew up in Ann Arbor, Michigan, and was educated at the University of Michigan and Stanford University. *Water Walker* is her eighth collection of poetry. In addition, she has published three collections of short stories and essays; a novel, *Things Invisible to See;* and several books for children. *A Visit to William Blake's Inn: Poems for Innocent and Experienced Travelers* won the Newbery Medal. She lives in Poughkeepsie, New York, with her husband, Eric Lindbloom, and teaches in the English department at Vassar College.

A Note on the Type

The text of this book was composed in a film version of Basilia, a type face designed in 1960 by Markus Low, a native of Lucerne, Switzerland. Low designed the capital letters first, basing them on the golden section. Four years later, he added the lower-case letters, making them conform optically rather than mathematically to the rhythm of the capitals.

Composed by the Sarabande Press, New York, New York. Printed and bound by Fairfield Graphics, Fairfield, Pennsylvania.
Designed by Virginia Tan